Welcome to the Performance Pack for 'The Shining, Signing Star'.

Inside this pack you will find everything that you need to prepare for your performance.

This pack contains not only the script and suggestions for enhancing your production, with tips for constructing props and costumes, but also a specially recorded CD of the songs plus video clips of the signs.

The CD has two versions of each of the songs, with and without vocals, so that your cast can either join in with the pre-recorded vocals or sing along to the fully orchestrated backing tracks.

Those who prefer to provide their own accompaniment are also catered for, as the pack contains the full piano / guitar and vocal score for all three original songs, which have been specially written and arranged by award winning composer, Paul K. Joyce.

Whatever style of production you choose to put on, whether it is a lavish, large scale epic with a huge cast, or something altogether smaller and simpler involving just a few children, everything that you need is here.

This pack contains:

- **Full cast list** - with icons to indicate those roles that are speaking and signing parts, together with suggestions for increasing or decreasing the number of acting roles in your production.

- **Props, Scenery & Costume notes** – Suggestions for the construction of the props, staging ideas and notes on costume and make –up for the play.

- **Six step plan** –Suggestions and notes to help guide you step by step from the first reading of the script, right through to the final performance.

- **Complete play script** - The full script for the play itself, in a format suitable to photocopy for distributing to your cast and crew of helpers.

- **Explanation of signs** – Full colour photographs and written instructions on how to produce all of the signs used in the play.

- **Piano / guitar and vocal score** – Full sheet music for the three, specially composed, original songs.

- **Enhanced CD** – Disc containing fully orchestrated versions of the overture and songs from the play both with and without pre–recorded guide vocal, together with video clips of how to produce each of the signs used in the play.

Contents

GW01392989

Foreword

by **Gervase Phinn**

The musical nativity play, 'The Shining, Signing Star', is a delight in all it contains.

With a wealth of characters, the superb and often moving script is easily accessible to both the deaf and hearing child and it must be a pleasure to perform.

I strongly recommend this lively and entertaining play which celebrates one of the greatest stories ever told.

Professor Gervase Phinn taught in a range of schools for fourteen years before becoming an education adviser and school inspector. He is now a freelance lecturer, broadcaster and writer.

He has published many articles, chapters and books and edited a wide range of poetry and short story collections. He is the bestselling author of many titles, including 'Classroom Creatures', 'It Takes One to Know One', 'The Day Our Teacher Went Batty' and 'A Wayne in a Manger'.

For more information visit **www.gervase-phinn.com**

Introduction

by **Garry Slack**

The nativity play is an annual event that takes place in many schools, nurseries, play groups and village halls all over the world.
I am sure that many of us have childhood memories of taking part in a show celebrating the Christmas story.

But, in fact, the nativity play is a tradition much older than many of us realise.

It is thought that St Francis of Assisi set up the first three dimensional nativity scene to celebrate Christmas as long ago as 1220 in the town of Greccio in Italy.

Although there were already drawings and paintings of the nativity, St Francis used real animals, including an ox and a donkey, to show people how the nativity would have looked.

By using live animals instead of just a painting, people were able to use all their senses to experience the scene for themselves, imagining what it must have been like to have been in that stable all those years ago.

Although most nativity plays no longer use real donkeys, once a year, many of us still gather together in school halls to watch children act out the familiar story of the birth of Jesus.

This play is my attempt to retell the story from the point of view of the animals as they journey from all over the world to view the baby Jesus, using signs and songs that can be easily learnt and enjoyed by everyone.

I very much hope that you enjoy this new version of the age old story.

........Follow the donkey!

How to use this pack

A word about the signs in the play

In the script for 'The Shining, Signing Star', you will notice that some of the words in the text are highlighted in red.

These key words are to be both spoken and signed at the same time.

Whenever you come across a red word, you will find that it corresponds to a sign in the 'Explanation of signs' section that starts before the script on page 17.

As you become familiar with the script, you will find that many of the signed words appear over and over again. This repetition will help you to learn both the script and the signs.

How many signs are there in the play?

The play contains over a hundred signs, which, to a newcomer to sign language, may seem like an awful lot. But, you don't have to use all of the signs if you don't want to.

Flexibility is the key to a successful production. The script and suggestions in this pack are intended as guidelines

This will be your production, so feel free to use as many or as few of the signs as you wish.

The signs used in this play have been chosen to enhance and compliment the spoken dialogue, and it's true that this show can even be performed without the signs, using only the dialogue.

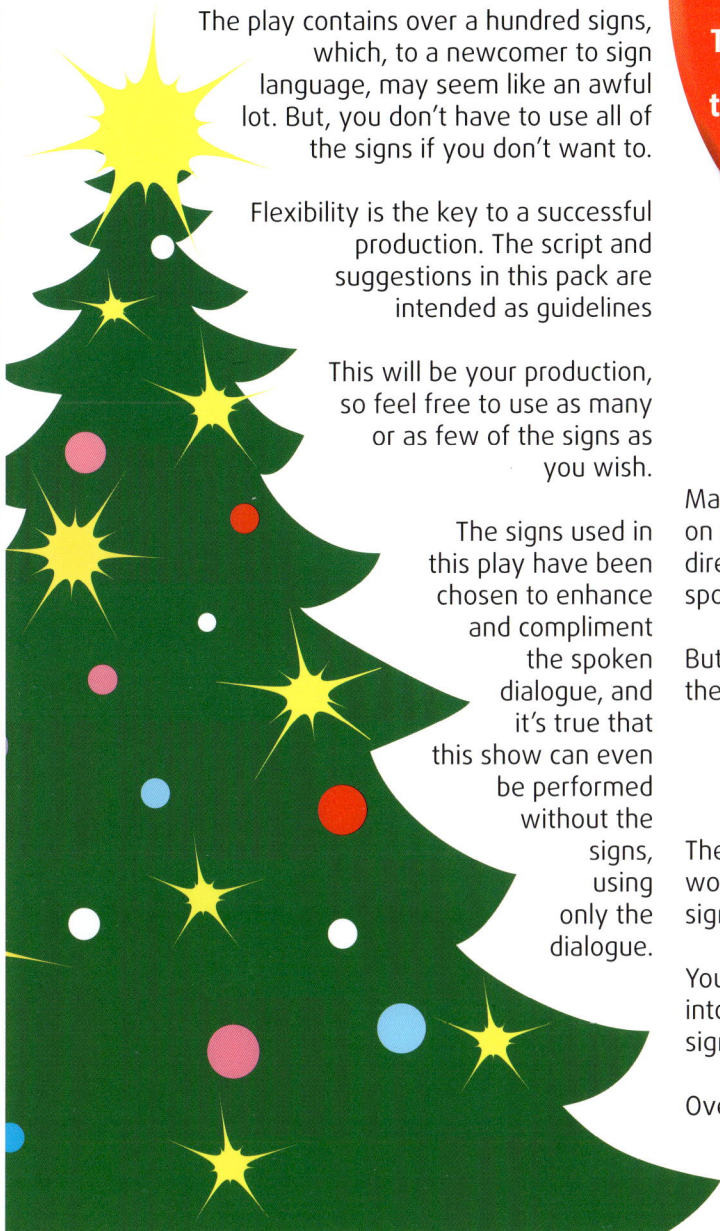

But, in all honesty, there can be few more heart-warming and uplifting sights than that of a group of children performing a signed song together; hands and voices working together in perfect harmony.

Sign language and songs were made for each other!

It is important to take plenty of time in the weeks leading up to your performance to practise the play and all the signs and songs.

Some children will learn the signs more quickly than others so try to be as patient as you can and keep repeating the signs, if possible, using them on a daily basis.

To help your group learn the signs, why not photograph yourself or the children doing the signs and put them up on the walls as a reminder?

If you have access to a video camera you could even video the children doing the signs.

Where do I begin?

Many people feel daunted just by the prospect of putting on an ordinary nativity play, so the idea of producing and directing a play that uses sign language as well as the spoken word may seem like too much to take on!

But don't worry; nobody is expecting you to memorise the signs and the script all in one go!

Five signs a day

The best way to get to grips with learning the signs is to work together as a group, learning perhaps just five new signs each day.

You could learn the signs in alphabetical order or turn it into a game by asking the children to randomly pick the signs to be learnt out of a hat.

Over a period of just five days it's possible to learn an amazing twenty five signs, that's nearly a quarter of the signs used in the play!

Sign a song

There is a long and established tradition of children learning songs that combine music with actions.

By learning a signed song it is possible to quickly build up a large vocabulary of signs whilst having fun at the same time.

'The Shining, Signing Star' has three specially written songs that combine words, music and signs.

To help you learn the songs you can use the accompanying CD that comes with this pack and sing along to the songs, or for those who prefer to use live music, this pack contains sheet music for piano or keyboards and guitar.

Many people find that learning the songs is the best way to familiarise themselves with the signs because each song contains the most frequently used signs.

In fact, the song 'Follow the Donkey' contains over forty of the signs used in the play!

Learning to sign will help the children to watch, think, listen and concentrate more closely on what is being taught.

You will be amazed at how quickly you, and the children, learn the signs and how eager they will be to learn more signs.

The Script

As you become more familiar with the signs you will see how easily they fit into the play.

To keep the narrative moving along and to maintain the children's attention, the script has been kept deliberately short and, as previously mentioned, many of the signs are repeated again and again throughout the play, and accompanying songs.

Because the play is written in rhyme, it makes it easy and enjoyable for children to learn and memorise – just as if they were learning the words to a song or rap!

Script to stage

Gradually, as your group increases its vocabulary of signs and begins to improve their signing skills, you can begin to incorporate the signs into the script as you rehearse the play ready for your performance.

BINGO!

Once you have learnt all the signs, why not test the children's knowledge by playing a game of signed Bingo!

It's easy to make your own Bingo cards - either on a computer or by using a pencil, pens, a ruler and some card.

For tips on making cards, search online for 'blank bingo cards'
Make enough Bingo cards for your players, choose the signs that you want to use to play the game, and then 'call' the game by making the signs for the players without using your voice.

Play first for a' line' and then a 'full house'.
The winners then have to sign the words back to you to confirm that they have recognised the signs correctly.

This is a great way of testing the children's vocabulary of signs and improving their concentration skills at the same time!

Casting your play

This play was originally written for a cast of forty five children.

Of those forty five parts, there are thirty seven roles that are speaking/signing parts and the remaining eight parts are supportive roles.

However, this play is designed to be as flexible as possible, so feel free to increase or decrease the parts to suit the number of performers that you have.

For example, the child carrying the placards that link together each scene appears eight times in the show. This part can either be played by the same child each time or by eight different children, or even by several children sharing the role. It's up to you – it's your production!

More....

As previously mentioned, there are forty five parts in the original script, but the cast list for this play can be expanded to accommodate more children.

By increasing the numbers of children playing the parts of the stars, doves and animals, you can really make this an epic performance – The only limitations are the size of your performing area!

....Or Less!

If, however, you have a limited number of children for the show, less than the forty five suggested in the script, it is still possible to perform the play.

By reducing the number of parts, particularly in the larger chorus groups of the animals, doves and stars and by getting children to 'double up' on some of the main roles, you can still go ahead and stage the play with as few as sixteen children.

Meanwhile, behind the scenes.....

For children who may not wish to perform on the stage, there are still plenty of opportunities for them to be involved in the production.

There are lots of things that they can help with, such as

• Making the props
• Painting the scenery
• Creating the costumes
• Face painting
• Designing posters and flyers to help publicise the show

Each of the animal groups - 'The Animals of the Forest', 'Sea' and 'Countryside' can be played by just one child with cardboard cut-outs or soft toys representing the other animals in the group.

Children can also 'double up' some of the other parts.

The four children at the start of the play, who portray the carol singers, could also play the parts of the innkeepers and doves as well.

Boy, Girl, Girl, Boy!

All of the characters in the show, with the exceptions of the three wise men and Mary and Joseph, can be played by either boys or girls. If you are short of boys to take part in the production, it is possible to ask a girl to play the part of Joseph and recast the three wise men as the three wise women!

Simply change the introductory line spoken and signed by the wise men from 'Kings with gold' to 'Queens with gold,' as the sign used for 'King' and 'Queen' is the same.

Safety in Numbers!

To reflect the fact that not every child feels confident enough to memorise and deliver lines and signs by themselves, there are passages in the play where various groups such as the animals, stars and entire cast speak and sign their lines together as a group.

Cast of characters

Casting a play is a big undertaking, so to help you choose your cast, each of the parts featured in the play are described below, together with an explanation of what is required for each role, whether the role is a walk on part with no dialogue or if it is a more challenging role that requires the child to speak and sign etc.

There are also suggestions on how the roles could be altered to accommodate larger or smaller productions.

To further help you, each character description has an icon next to it to indicate what type of role it is.

In this play the children who are part of the cast are required to do a variety of things:

- Speak and sign dialogue, both alone and as a group.
- Sing & sign songs as a group
- Mime actions and signs
- Play a character

Placard Carrier

This is a non—speaking, non—signing role. The placard carrier appears eight times in the show and helps to link the scenes together by carrying large placards with jokey captions that tell the audience where each scene is set.
For smaller productions this part can be performed by just one child or increased to eight walk on parts for a larger cast.
Recommended number = 1

First, Second, Third and Fourth Carol Singers

These are speaking and signing roles with one line each.
These children are present day carol singers who are on their way home on a cold Christmas Eve.
For smaller productions these parts can be shared between two children.
Recommended number = 4

First Star, Second Star, Third Star, Fourth Star and Fifth Star

These are speaking and signing roles with one line each, plus shared dialogue and songs with other characters.
These are the magical silver stars that have looked down from the sky and watched events on Earth since Christmas began.
If you only have a small cast, these roles can be shared between two or three children.
For larger productions it is possible to increase the number of stars on stage by using more children.
Recommended number = 5

First Dove, Second Dove, Third Dove and Fourth Dove

These are speaking and signing roles with one line each, plus shared dialogue and songs with other characters.
The doves are wise, regal birds that have been sent down from Heaven with an important message for the animal kingdom.
If you only have a small cast, these roles can be shared between two or three children.
For larger productions it is possible to increase the number of doves on stage, making them part of the chorus.
Recommended number = 4

The Golden Star

This is a speaking and signing role with two solo lines, plus shared dialogue and songs with other characters.
The Golden Star is the Shining, Signing Star of the title. He or She is the brightest and most magical star in the sky with a very important job to do.
Recommended number = 1

Donkey

This is a speaking and signing role with one solo line, plus shared dialogue and songs with other characters.
Although he may not be the most glamorous or cleverest creature, The donkey is very proud to be chosen as the animal who leads the creatures of the Earth to see the baby Jesus in Bethlehem.
Recommended number = 1

The Animals of the Forest

This is a shared speaking and signing role with one line spoken and signed as a group, plus shared dialogue and songs with other characters.
The Animals of the Forest include creatures such as badgers, bats, foxes etc.

Key to the symbols

A speaking and signing role.

A shared speaking and signing role where several characters speak and sign the lines together as a group.

A non—speaking role with signing only.

A non—speaking, non—signing role.

For small productions this role can be taken by just one child. For larger productions you can increase the number of animals to accommodate as many children as you wish.
Recommended number = 4

The Animals of the Sea

This is a shared speaking and signing role with one line spoken and signed as a group, plus shared dialogue and songs with other characters.

The Animals of the Sea include fish, seals, crabs, sea birds etc.

For small productions this role can be taken by just one child. For larger productions you can increase the number of animals to accommodate as many children as you wish.
Recommended number = 4

The Animals of the Countryside

This is a shared speaking and signing role with one line spoken and signed as a group, plus shared dialogue and songs with other characters.

The Animals of the Countryside include farm animals such as pigs, goats, cats and dogs etc.

For small productions this role can be taken by just one child. For larger productions you can increase the number of animals to accommodate as many children as you wish.
Recommended number = 4

The Three Innkeepers

These are non–speaking roles, that only require the children to shake their heads and make the sign for 'sorry'.

The Three Innkeepers should be able to mime and look sad as they turn Mary and Joseph away from their Inns.

These parts could be played by cast members who are also playing other parts in the show such as the Carol Singers.
Recommended number = 3

The Fourth Innkeeper

This is a speaking and signing role, with two solo lines, plus shared dialogue and songs

with other characters.

This Innkeeper is at first a bit gruff, telling Mary and Joseph to 'go away'. But he or she soon has a change of heart and offers the couple lodgings in his stable.

This part could be played by a cast member who is also playing another part in the show.
Recommended number = 1

Mary

This is a speaking and signing role, with three solo lines, plus shared dialogue and songs with other characters.

Mary is one of the more traditional characters in the play. She is a strong character who wants the best for her baby and is not afraid to tell the assembled animals to 'pipe down' when they get too noisy!
Recommended number = 1

> **Look Mum! It's me!**
> As well as the main roles that use sign and speech, there are also parts in the play, such as the placard carriers, or the sheep paparazzi, that require no signing, speaking or singing, which may suit those children who are a little shyer.

Joseph

This is a speaking and signing role, with two solo lines, plus shared dialogue and songs with other characters.

Also a traditional character, Joseph is a proud parent who is desperate to get the best for his wife and baby.
Recommended number = 1

The Three Wise Men

This is a shared speaking and signing role with one solo line spoken and signed as a group, plus shared dialogue and songs with other characters.

Unlike the characters usually portrayed in nativity plays, the wise men in this play are more like celebrities or film stars, paying homage to the baby and showering him with lavish gifts.

These parts could be played by cast members who are also playing other parts in the show.
Recommended number = 3

The Three Shepherds

This is a shared speaking and signing role with one solo line spoken and signed as a group, plus shared dialogue and songs with other characters.

The shepherds are poor, honest people who don't have much to bring the baby in the way of fancy gifts, like the wise men. Nevertheless, they come with good hearts and love. These parts could be played by cast members who are also playing other parts in the show.
Recommended number = 3

The Sheep Paparazzi

This is a non–speaking, non–signing role. The children are required to rush onto the stage and take 'photographs' of Mary, Joseph and the baby.

The Sheep Paparazzi are a noisy bunch of reporters and photographers who just happen to be sheep! They are not averse to pushing one another out of the way in order to get the best photograph or interview for their particular magazine.

For smaller productions this part can be performed by just one child. For larger productions you can increase the number of paparazzi.
Recommended number = 4

Mouse

This is a speaking and signing role with one solo line, plus shared dialogue and songs with other characters.

Like all mice, Mouse is a timid and shy creature, but eventually his or her patience is pushed to the limit by the paparazzi blocking the view!

This part could be played by a cast member who is also playing another part in the show.
Recommended number = 1

Rehearsal tips

In order to achieve your goal of a successful show, rehearsals need to be carefully planned and structured, but they also need to be a fun experience for the children taking part. Take time to plan each rehearsal in advance and remember to have fun together as a team.

• Plan when and where you will rehearse and how long each practice session will take. Get a calendar and clearly mark every rehearsal and performance on it or make a poster and write 'Days until the show' on it, counting down the days one by one until the performance.

• Be aware of holidays and other dates when people may not be able to attend rehearsals.

• Get parents involved. Parents can work at home with their children to help them memorise their lines and signs.

• During rehearsals create a signal to get the children's attention. This could be something like clapping your hands, shaking a tambourine or quickly flicking the room lights on and off.

• Have a plan B. Every production will have its setbacks, so always have another plan up your sleeve. Consider what you would do if a child was unable to perform due to illness, or how you would cope if the sound system broke down or the person playing the piano didn't turn up for the performance.

• To make the experience fun, introduce simple drama games, such as mirroring each others actions or miming various tasks. These fun games will help the children to get used to acting out a role. (See below)

• Both acting, and sign language, involves the use of facial expression. Get the children to practise showing different emotions and expressions and applying them to their character. For example, the donkey in the play is proud to be leading the animals to Bethlehem, whilst the Golden Star is wise and has seen many things. How would the children show this in their faces?

Charades

This simple drama game will help the children get into character and improve their acting skills.

Split the group into two teams, team A and team B.

Give each team several slips of paper. On each slip of paper the teams should write down the names of a famous book, film, television programme, song, or phrase. Each team then puts their slips of paper into a separate box in front of them.

A player from Team A draws a slip from Team B's box and looks at the paper. That player then has three minutes to act out the title on the paper for his or her team mates without using their voice.

The player starts by indicating what category the title is in, (book, film etc) and how many words are in the phrase. Then he or she can either act out the words one at a time or try to act out the whole title in one go.

Categories:
• **Book title:** Unfold your hands as if they were opening a book.
• **Film:** Pretend to crank an old-fashioned movie camera.
• **Play:** mime pulling open the curtains of a theatre.
• **Song:** Throw out your arms and pretend to sing.
• **TV programme:** Draw a rectangle to outline the TV screen.
• **Phrase:** Make quotation marks in the air with your fingers.

You, as the timekeeper, must keep watch of the time and tell the player when the three minutes is up.
If the player's team guess correctly within the three minutes then they win a point. If they do not guess it in the time, then the point goes to the other team.

Next, a player from Team B draws a phrase slip from Team A's box, and play continues.
The game continues until every player has had a go. The team with the highest score wins the game.

Props, scenery & costume suggestions

Putting on a production means working together as a team to find and create the various items that are needed for the show.

Even children who have no interest in performing on the stage can really get involved with the different creative and artistic activities that are required for a production.

It is perfectly possible to perform this play with the minimum of props and scenery. But, part of the fun in putting on a performance is in creating all the various items that help make the show come to life.

For many children this will be their first contact with drama and the theatre, so this is a great opportunity for them to learn, not only about the importance of working together as a team, but also to discover that a show is not just about what happens on stage. Just as much hard work goes on behind the scenes.

It is very important for children to understand that the performers and the backstage crew must work together in order to make the show a success.

Props

Remember that as this production uses sign language it is important that any props are freestanding or can be put down if the character holding them is required to sign.

The props featured in the play include;

Lanterns

Each of the four carol singers at the start of the show are carrying lanterns.

In order to be able to sign, the children will need to put the lanterns down onto the floor.

The lanterns can be the hurricane type that can usually be bought from camping stores or they can be Chinese style lanterns made from cardboard and paper.

Tavern Signs

Each of the four innkeepers will need a large board depicting the name of the tavern that they own.

The boards should be colourful, with large lettering that can be easily read by the audience. The boards will also need to be free standing to enable the innkeepers to have both hands free for signing.

Apart from the standard inn names such as 'The Green Dragon'' or 'The White Horse', the children can have fun making up their own names and artwork for each of the taverns.

The name of the fourth tavern could be something that fits in with the story such as 'The Shining, Star' or 'The Talking Hands'.

Scenery

This play can be staged with the minimum of scenery because the placards that appear in each scene help to describe where the action is taking place.

But, to give the play more atmosphere, you can create backcloths for each scene. These can be painted onto old sheets or roller blinds and hung up at the back of the performance area.

Scene 1: Christmas Eve in a modern day town
Paint the silhouettes of buildings against a wintery night sky, with the moon and stars high above the town.

Scene 2: The night sky
This can be the same backcloth that was used in scene 1, or you could paint a space scene featuring the Milky Way, stars and planets with the edge of the earth visible at the bottom of the backcloth.

Scene 3: In a meadow
The sun is high in the sky and looking down on a green landscape with a road winding out of sight over the hills. A signpost is pointing towards Bethlehem.

Scene 4: Bethlehem
A painting of the night sky above the old town of Bethlehem. A dimly lit stable could be shown in the centre of the backcloth.

1

CHRISTMAS EVE.

SALES START 10.00 AM BOXING DAY

2

MEANWHILE,

UP ABOVE....

3

GOING BACK IN TIME NOW...

...HOLD ON TIGHT!

4

A LONG TIME AGO, IN A MEADOW FAR, FAR AWAY...

Placards

Eight placards are needed for the show.

They need to be large enough for the audience to read but light enough for a child to carry.

It is possible to make the placards from large sheets of cardboard and construct them so that they hang around the child's neck like a 'sandwich board' or, alternatively, make large signs that can be easily carried across the stage.

The writing on each placard needs to be legible and large enough to be read by members of the audience at the back of the hall.

5

BETHLEHEM 500 MILES

WELCOME BREAK 2 MILES

6

WELCOME TO BETHLEHEM.

(NO VACANCIES)

HAVE A NICE DAY!

7

BLEAT MAGAZINE EXCLUSIVE!

AT HOME WITH MARY, JOSEPH AND THEIR BEAUTIFUL NEW BABY BOY!

8

THE END.

(APPLAUSE PLEASE)

The Crib

The crib could be a painted cardboard box, a Moses basket or toy cot brought in from home.

The Baby

A toy baby, suitably wrapped in a blanket, could be used.

Cameras for the sheep paparazzi

You can use either old cameras brought in from home, toy cameras, or even make your own old fashioned style paparazzi cameras, using cereal boxes for the camera body and kitchen rolls for the lens. Some of the sheep should also carry small note pads and pencils.

Costumes

Traditionally, nativity costumes have been made from items that can be found in most households, such as dressing gowns, ponchos and of course the obligatory tea towels sported by the shepherds in practically every nativity play there has ever been!

Of course, depending on your production, you can carry on this fine and ancient custom, but with a little thought and effort you can really make your production stand out from the crowd!

Remember that you don't have to do all the work yourself.

Get your helpers to put the word out to parent's and other adults that you are looking for costumes for a nativity play. Send out a newsletter asking for donations of suitable clothing or material.

Don't forget to mention that if any of the parents are handy with a needle and thread that you'd love to hear from them!

The important thing to remember when choosing costumes for this particular play is that because this play contains sign language, the costumes need to allow for free and unrestricted movement of the arms and hands.

Try to keep in mind that sign language is a gestural language so the actors' movements must not be restricted by their costumes.

Below are some ideas and suggestions for costumes and make up to add a little extra magic to your show, but why not let your imagination run wild and add ideas of your own to give your production a really unique look!

Placard Carrier

The placards link the scenes together with humorous messages that help the audience know where each scene is taking place.

Depending on the overall look of your production, there are lots of possibilities for the costumes of the placard carriers. The children playing the carriers can be simply dressed in a dark coloured t-shirt and trousers so as not to detract from the slogan on the placard or you could have them wearing brightly coloured clothes like royal messengers or even dressed as angels. The choice is yours!

First, Second, Third and Fourth Carol Singer

The children in the opening scene of the play are dressed as carol singers on their way home on a cold winters night. These children could be dressed in modern clothes with coats, hats, scarves and gloves to keep out the winter chill.

First Star, Second Star, Third Star, Fourth Star, and Fifth Star

The children playing the shining stars need to be dressed in silvery costumes that catch and reflect the light.

One way of doing this is to have the children dressed all in black or dark blue to represent the night sky and then make a kind of star shaped sandwich board that goes over the child's shoulders.

Start by cutting two big star shapes out of large sheets of cardboard. Cover them in tin foil or paint them silver and sprinkled them with glitter or tiny mirror sequins so that they really sparkle.

Remember that as these are both speaking and signing roles the children will need to be able to move their hands and arms freely.

The cardboard star shapes are then held together by punching two small holes through either side of the top part of the stars and threading silver coloured ribbon or string through the holes and securing it with a knot at the back.

The stars are then draped over the child's shoulders, one at the front and one at the back. To make sure that the stars stay in place, thread more ribbon through the front and back of the stars and tie together at the sides.

Alternatively, it is possible to buy star costumes from shops or search on the internet for simple ways of making nativity costumes.

First Dove, Second Dove, Third Dove, and Fourth Dove

The doves could be dressed in white with yellow shoes if possible. If you can't find yellow shoes, you could make yellow cardboard 'feet' that can be taped over the children's own shoes.

To suggest the beaks of the doves, try using white baseball caps, covering the peaks of the caps in yellow fabric.

Glue two white pompoms onto the top of the cap for the eyes, remembering to glue black cardboard circles onto the pompoms to represent the pupils of the eyes.

In addition to creating costumes, you might want to enhance to the look of your production by using masks or face paints for some of the characters, particularly the stars and animals.

It is important to be aware that sign language not only uses the hands to communicate, but facial expressions also help to put across the message, so try not to use anything that would distort the facial expressions too much.

If you choose to use masks, make sure that you don't use full face masks as they might not only muffle the children's voices but they could also obscure their lips, making it difficult for any member of the audience who relied on lip reading to be able to understand what was being said.

A simple and cheap way of making your own animal heads is to draw templates for the animals' heads, photocopy them, stick them to cardboard and then paint them.
Next, staple them to a band of card which you can fasten around the children's' heads.

Face paints are a very effective way of creating a strong visual look for a character.
Make sure to only use paints specially designed for face painting and follow all the health and safety advice for safe use of the paints, making sure that you have parental permission and that the children have no skin allergies or infections.

The Golden Star

The Golden Star's costume can be made in the same way as the costumes for the other stars, except that it should be coloured gold and be a much grander and more sparkly costume than the other stars.

Donkey

A grey hooded sweatshirt and jogging bottoms could be worn together with black shoes for the hooves. To make the ears, follow the tip in the circle below.

The tail can be made by attaching a strip of grey material, or cord with a black fringe, to the back of the jogging bottoms.

The Animals of the Forest

The Animals of the Forest include creatures such as badgers, bats, foxes etc.

All of these costumes can be achieved by the children being dressed in sweatshirts and jogging bottoms in the colour of the animals – brown for a bear, black for a bat etc – topped off with appropriate ears and possibly with faces painted in the style of the animal. (See circle right and tips box on page 12)

Tails can be made from strips of material or by stuffing long socks and attaching them to the back of the jogging bottoms.

The Animals of the Sea

The Animals of the Sea include fish, seals, crabs, sea birds etc.

One idea is to dress the children in blue and green to represent the colours of the sea, wearing headbands with cardboard fish, covered in silver paper attached to them.

Or, alternatively, you could cut out lots of shiny fish shapes and attach them to blue t-shirts to represent a school of fish.

For a crab construct a costume shell in the same way that you made the star outfits. Paint it red and make the eyes from suitably painted ping pong balls stapled to drinking straws and attached to a headband.

The Animals of the Countryside

The Animals of the Countryside include farm animals such as pigs, goats, cats and dogs etc.

All of these costumes can be achieved by the children being dressed in sweatshirts and jogging bottoms in the colour of the animals – brown for a dog, pink for a pig, black for a cat etc. – topped off with appropriate ears and possibly with faces painted in the style of the animal. (See tips box on page 12)

Tails can be made from strips of material or by stuffing long socks and attaching them to the back of the jogging bottoms.

> A simple, but effective way of making animal ears for your costumes is to draw the shape and size of the ears that you want onto cardboard, leaving a small tab of card at the bottom of the pattern that can be used to fix the ears in place with later.
>
> Carefully cut out your ear shapes and then cover them with the appropriate colour of felt. Cut out a smaller triangle of felt in a lighter colour to represent the inside of the ears. Glue these smaller inner ear shapes onto the large ears.
>
> Fold the tab at the bottom of each of the ears up and then use a glue gun to attach the ears by the tabs to a head band.
>
> Using this method you will easily be able to make ears for all sorts of animals such as foxes, kangaroos, cats and pigs!

The Innkeepers

The Innkeepers should look like tavern owners.

As there are four of them, it might be a good idea to dress them in contrasting colours. Try long t-shirts with rolled up sleeves, jeans and heavy work boots. Each innkeeper should also wear a plain apron.

Mary

Mary could be in a plain white dress or robe with a blue shawl or pashmina for a head—dress which can be held in place with a headband.

Joseph

Joseph is a carpenter and could be plainly dressed in a long brown t-shirt with a dressing gown or tunic tied up with a belt or length of cord.

Alternatively, if you wanted a more modern day look for your production, you could dress Joseph as a builder with hard hat, check shirt, jeans and work boots!

The Three Wise Men

The wise men in this play should look like Hollywood film stars.

Try dressing them in flashy, expensive looking gear with plenty of bling!

If you prefer a more classic movie star, you could opt for a sophisticated look and dress them in white towelling dressing gowns with cravats and slicked back hair.

Whichever look you opt for, don't forget the sunglasses to shield their eyes from the flash guns of the paparazzi!

The Three Shepherds

The shepherds are much poorer than the wise men and their clothes should reflect this.

Ripped jeans and work shirts could be used, plus of course the obligatory tea towel head wear!

Sew patches of different coloured cloth onto the knees and elbows of their outfits to indicate that their clothes have seen better days and been repaired many times.

The Sheep Paparazzi

A quick sheep costume can be made using a white t-shirt or white woolly jumper with black tights or leggings.

Add a pair of cardboard ears, covered with white felt attached to a headband.

Some of the sheep will be armed with cameras while others will carry a note pad for that exclusive scoop!

Mouse

Make the ears for the mouse in the same way that you would for the other animals.

Dress him or her in either a grey or brown sweatshirt with matching jogging bottoms.

Make a tail from a long strip of suitably coloured material.

Use face paints to give your mouse a nose and whiskers.

Step by step to showtime!

Ok, so you've agreed to produce the nativity play.

That should be no problem, you think to yourself. After all, Christmas is a long way away.......

Then suddenly panic sets in, as you realise that showtime is closer than you think!

Relax! Just follow this simple six step plan and you will soon have the children treading the boards like seasoned professionals!

Step 1

· Get to know all about the play by reading through all the material in this pack.

· Keep a notebook with you at all times so that you can jot down any ideas that you may have relating to the show. It might be a good idea to divide your notebook into different sections such as 'Props', 'Costume', 'Music' etc., so that you can make notes under the appropriate headings and find them again easily when you need to refer back to them.

· Get yourself an assistant director and several pairs of helping hands. There is a lot of work involved in putting on a production so accept any offer of help!

· Make copies of the script and hand them out to your helpers.

· Decide on when and where you will perform the play.

Step 2

· Introduce the idea of the play to the children.

· Discuss the different characters in the play with the children. Ask who might be interested in being in the play or helping backstage.

· To stimulate an interest in sign language in your group, you could ask them to think of all the different ways in which people communicate. Perhaps you could spend a session teaching them about sign language. For example, you could teach the children how to finger spell the alphabet and their own names. Look on the Internet for 'BSL finger spelling alphabet' and you should easily be able to find a copy of the alphabet to work with.

Step 3

· Decide on your cast. Remember that you can adapt the number of parts to suit the needs of your group.

· Hand out copies of the script to your cast. Encourage parents to help with learning lines at home.

· Put the word out to parents and other adults that you are looking for suitable costumes and props for the play. Don't forget to let it be known that any offers of help with making costumes etc. will be gratefully received!

Step 4

· Rehearse the script and signs, (see 'How to use this pack' on page 4 for hints on learning the songs and signs). It is important to not only practise as often as possible as a group, but also to encourage the children to practise at home with the help of family and friends.

· Use the CD in the pack to practise the signed songs. If you are using live musicians remember to include them in your rehearsal schedule.

· To ensure that rehearsals don't become too boring, remember to include some drama games. (See 'Rehearsal tips' on page 9)

· Those children who are part of the backstage crew can help to design and make the scenery, props, and posters to advertise the show.

Step 5

· Make sure that you have at least one full dress rehearsal. Everyone needs to treat the dress rehearsal it as if it were a real performance. This is a great opportunity to check that the costumes fit properly and that any last minute problems can be put right before the first performance.

Step 6

· The big day has finally arrived! The children are bound to be a little bit nervous so try to calm those nerves by warming up backstage with one of the signed songs.

Reassure them that you will be there to prompt them if they forget any of their lines or signs.

Check that the stage is set up ready for the first scene.

Remind them to smile and enjoy themselves, because it's ....

……….**Showtime!**

Helpful hand shapes

Sometimes it can be difficult to describe in a book how a particular sign is made or in what position the hands should be.

To make it easier for you to produce a sign there are several common hand shapes that occur frequently in sign language.

When you are looking at the explanation of a sign you may notice that sometimes they refer to things like a "Full C hand" or a "Bunched hand". Whenever you see these, or any other hand shapes referred to, use the pictures to the right to help you to produce the sign accurately.

Below is an example of how signs are presented in the vocabulary sections of the book. The direction of movement is shown by the red arrows on the vocabulary pictures. Double arrowheads indicate where two, repeat movements are required. Lines capping arrows show that the movement stops abruptly.

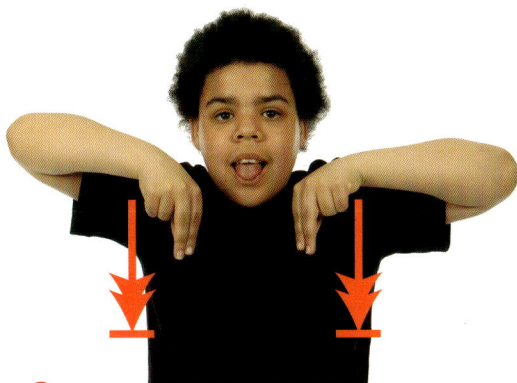

Dog
Two 'N' hands pointing down, make two, small downwards movements.

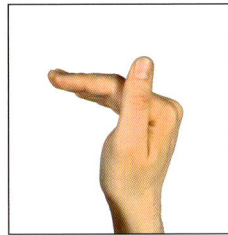
Bent Hand

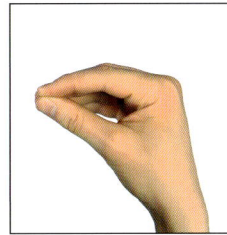
Bunched Hand

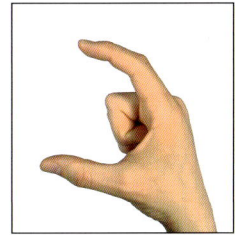
'C' Hand

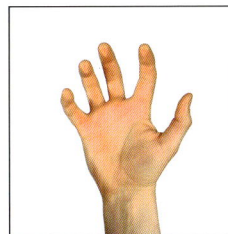
Clawed Hand

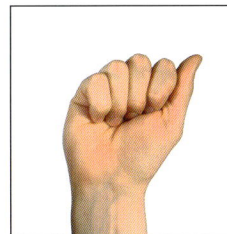
Closed Hand

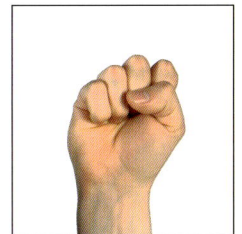
Fist

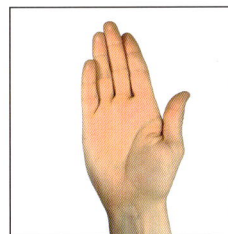
Flat Hand

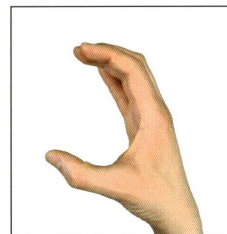
Full 'C' Hand

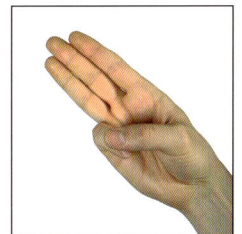
'M' Hand

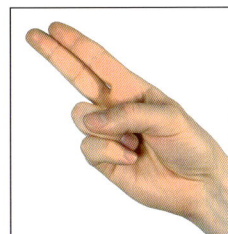
'N' Hand

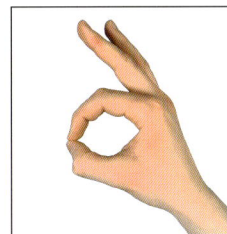
'O' Hand

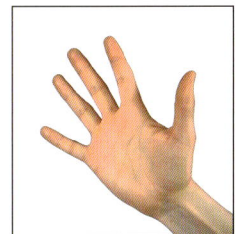
Open Hand

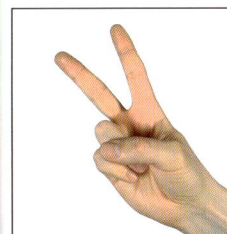
'V' Hand

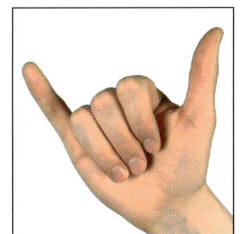
'Y' Hand

Left or right?

Lots of people get confused about whether they should sign with their left or right hand.

Generally one hand is more dominant than the other. This can be either the left or right hand. If you are comfortable with both, then it all depends on your own personal preference. The dominant hand is the one that you would normally write with and you should use this hand to sign with.

All of the photographs and descriptions in this book are shown and described from a right handed person's perspective. If you are left handed simply reverse the instructions.

Explanation of signs

Afar / Far / Far away / Travel
Hand, with index finger and thumb extended points into the distance and makes small circling movements.

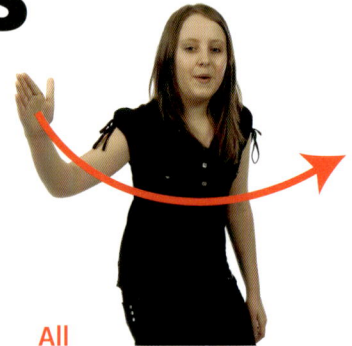

Above / Heaven
Hold both hands above the head, with the palms facing downwards and move them slowly apart whilst looking up to the sky.

All
'Open' hand, with the palm facing sideways, moves across the front of your body in a sweeping arc.

Animals
With 'clawed' hands, palms facing downwards make small forward movements as though creeping through the jungle.

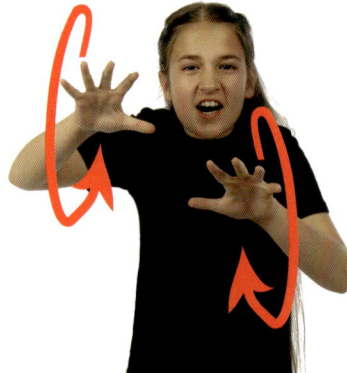

Asleep
Thumbs and index fingers of both hands slowly close at the sides of the eyes to mimic the eyelids closing.

Angels
Hold both hands in front of your chest with the palms facing you and cross them at the wrists to look like the wings of an angel. Wiggle your fingers.

Badger
A full 'C' hand, with fingers pointing downwards, moves over the front of the head, towards the back to indicate the white stripe on a badgers' head.

Bat
Index finger of one hand is pointing outwards horizontally to represent the branch of a tree, whilst the index and middle fingers of the other hand hook over the 'branch' to show how a bat hangs upside down.

Baby ('s)
Mime cradling a baby and gently rock your arms from side to side.

Beauty (Two Part Sign)
The fingertips of one hand touch together to form an 'O' shape at the lips and then spring open and move forwards away from the face.

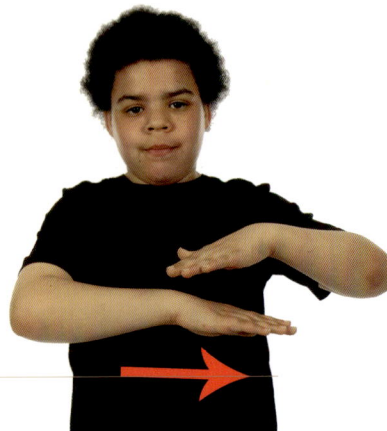

Beneath
Hold one 'flat' hand, with the palm facing downwards and then move the other 'flat' hand, with the palm also facing downwards, underneath it.

Bethlehem (Two part sign)
Fingerspell the letter 'B' and then a 'clawed' hand with the fingers pointing downwards, makes a short downward movement to indicate the sign for 'town'.

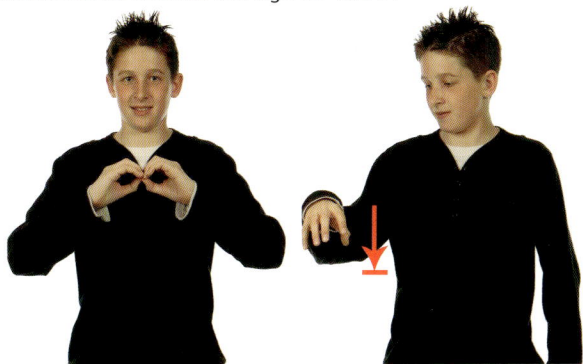

Bow / Bowed
Hold one arm flat across the front of the waist and bow forwards from the waist.

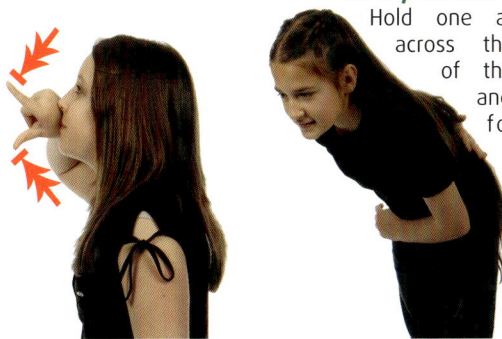

Birds / Doves
Open and close the index finger and the thumb near the mouth to imitate a bird's beak.

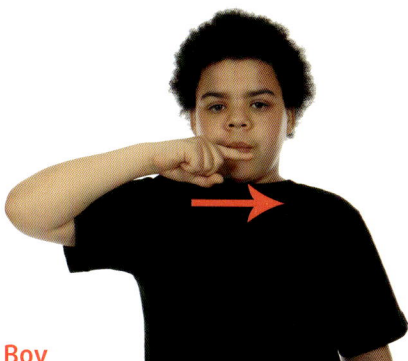

Boy
The outstretched index finger of the right hand points left and then moves from right to left just beneath the lower lip.

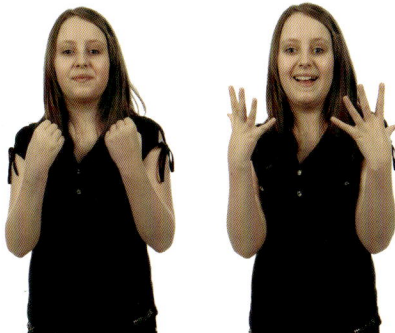

Bright (Two part sign)
Two bunched hands held in front of the body, with the palms facing towards the body, move quickly upwards as the fingers spring apart.

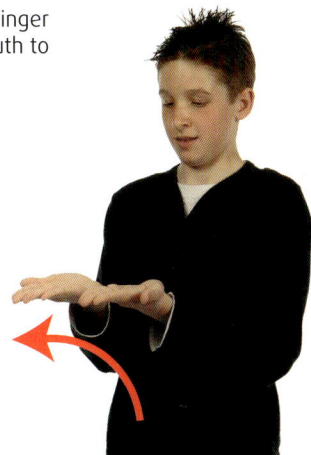

Bring / Bringer / Gift / Set before
Two flat hands, together with palms facing upwards, move forwards away from the body as if giving someone a gift.

Came
Outstretched index finger pointing upwards, held away from the body, moves back in the direction of the body.

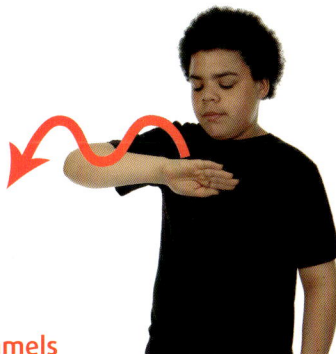

Camels
Use your 'flat' hand, with palm facing downwards, to describe the outline of the humps of a camel.

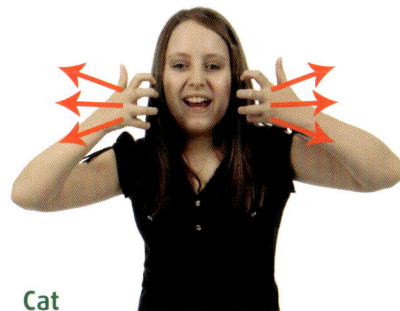

Cat
Flex the fingers of 'clawed hands' which move out and away from either side of the face to show whiskers.

Celebrate
Two 'Y' shape hands held upright on either side of the head, move in small circles.

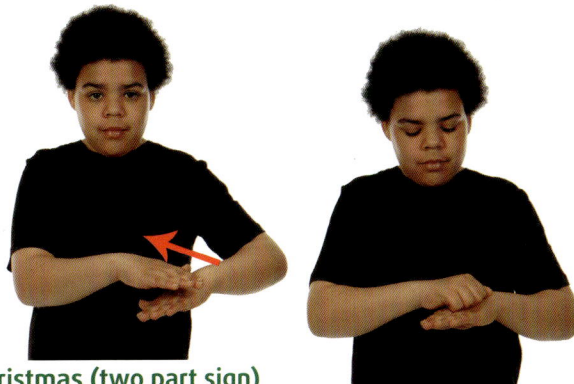

Christmas (two part sign)
Hold a left 'flat' hand with palm facing downwards. The right 'flat' hand with palm also facing downwards brushes back across the back of the left hand and then the fingers close into a 'fist' coming to rest on the back of the left hand.

Cold
With both hands 'closed' at either side of the chest, mime as if you are shivering with the cold.

Come on / Come
Signed the same as 'came' but it can also be signed by using the whole hand in a beckoning motion.

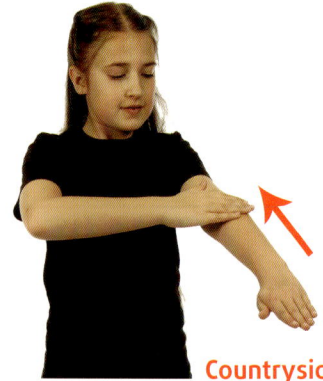

Countryside
The 'flat' right hand with palm facing downwards, sweeps up the outstretched right arm from the wrist towards the elbow.

Cows
Place 'Y' shaped hands on either side of the head with the thumbs touching the temples to show the horns of a cow.

Crab
Open and close the thumb and index fingers of both hands and move them across the body to indicate a crab's pincers opening and closing as it walks sideways.

Danger
'Flat' hand, with the palm facing to the left, taps twice against the forehead.

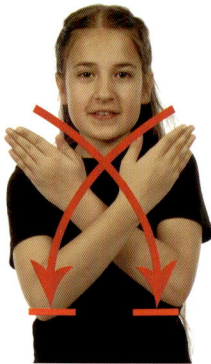

Dark / Night / Tonight
With both hands 'flat', pointing upwards and the palms facing towards you, swing your hands downwards so that they cross each other and end up across your body at waist height.

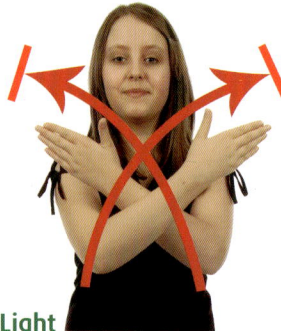

Day / Light
Start with both arms crossed with the palms facing towards your body at waist height. Now swing your hands upwards so that they cross each other and end up at either side of your face.

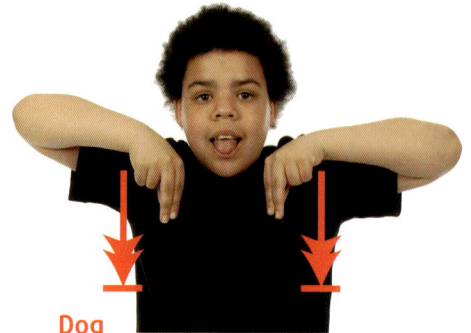

Dog
Two 'N' hands pointing down, make two, small downwards movements.

Donkey
Mime donkey's ears by placing two 'Flat' hands, with palms facing forward, on the top of your head and twitch them forwards twice.

Don't
Begin with your hands crossed at the wrists with both hands in a 'Flat' hand shape with palms facing downwards. Quickly move them apart whilst shaking your head.

Door
Left arm held horizontally across the body. Right arm in same horizontal position in front of left, slams shut from the right hand side of the body onto the left arm to mimic the closing of a door.

Down below
Index finger points down towards the ground.

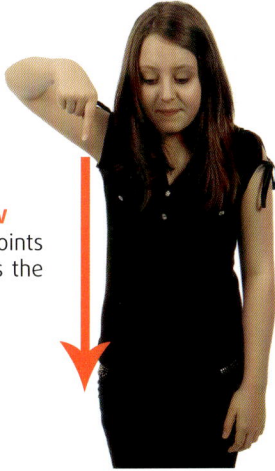

Each
Hand, with index finger pointing upwards, moves in front of the body from one side to the other in quick forward movements.

East
A 'Flat' right hand pointing upwards with the palm facing to the left, moves to the right to show the location of east on a compass.

Elephants
A full 'C' hand moves down and away from the nose in an arc to describe the shape of an elephant's trunk.

Enjoy / Happy / Joy
Both 'Flat' hands are held horizontally to the body with palms facing and hands slightly apart. The right hand then claps against the left as it brushes up the hand towards the left wrist, twice.

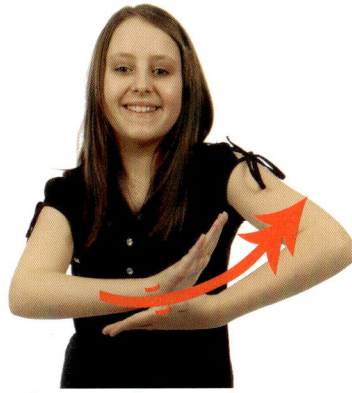

Every year
Both index fingers, pointing towards each other, roll forwards in small circles away from the body.

Feast
The bunched fingers of both hands move alternately back and forwards, towards the mouth as if putting food to the lips.

First / Once
Hold up your index finger in front of you to indicate the number one.

Fish
'Flat' hand moves forward across the body, twisting slightly at the wrist, in a swimming motion.

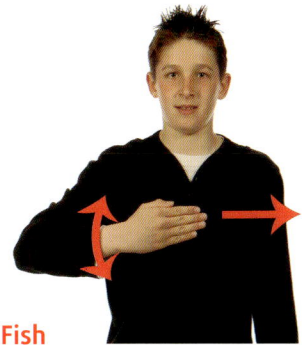

Follow / Following / Guided / Guide the way / Lead the way
Left hand, with index finger pointing horizontally away from the body and right hand with index finger also pointing horizontally, move forward and away from the body with the right hand following behind the left.

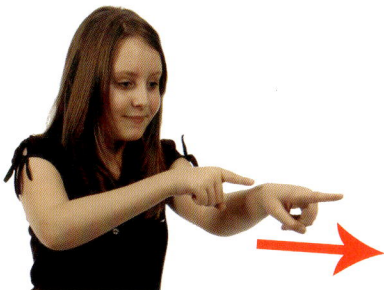

Forest
The elbow of the right arm rests on the back of the left hand. The fingers of the right hand represent the branches of a tree. The whole shape then moves slightly to the right and forwards in an arc to indicate more than one tree.

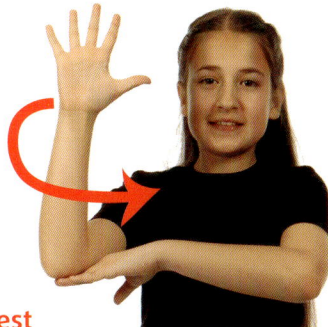

Fox
Fingers pointing towards the face, move away from the nose into a 'bunched' hand to show the shape of a fox's snout.

Full
Both 'flat' hands with palms facing down. Left hand is held above the right. The right hand moves upwards to make contact with the underside of the left.

Girl
With index finger pointing upwards and palm facing forwards, brush the finger down the side of the cheek twice.

Go
Point your index finger away from you in the direction you are talking about.

Gold / Golden (two part sign)
Fists bang together to finger spell the letter 'G' then fingers spring open as the hands move apart.

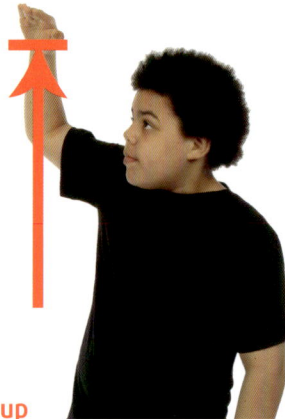

Grow up
Flat hand with palm facing downwards, moves upwards to indicate the height of a growing child.

Hear
Cup a hand to your ear as if listening for something.

Hello
Wave Hello.

Help / Helped
Fist with thumb extended upwards, rests on the flat open palm of the other hand and both hands move forwards or backwards depending on the context – 'you help me' or 'I help you'.

Hope
Hold up your hand and cross your index and middle fingers.

I / Me
Point to yourself.

Kangaroo
Hold your hands in front of you, close to your body, in the shape of a kangaroo's front paws and gently bounce them up and down as if you were hopping.

King (s)
Using a 'clawed hand shape,' gently touch the top of your head with your fingertips to show putting on a crown.

Know
Make your hand into a fist with your thumb sticking out. Hold your hand against the side of your head so that the thumb is touching your head.

Late

Use one 'flat' hand with the palm facing away from you to represent the face of a clock. With your other hand, hold out just your index finger and thumb. These are the hands of the clock. The tip of the thumb touches the palm of the left hand as the index finger moves quickly down in an arc to show the hands going around the clock.

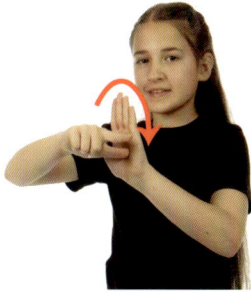

Long ago / Long, long ago

Flat hands held above the shoulder with the palms facing backwards; make backwards circles over the shoulder to show the years rolling back and the passage of time.

Look / See / Watch / Watched

The fingers of a 'V' hand move forward and away from the eye.

Looked down / Looking down

Both hands with the index and middle fingers in a 'V' shape are held above and to either side of the head with the fingers pointing forwards to represent two pairs or eyes. The hands twist forwards at the wrist so that the 'eyes' look down. At the same time the head should tilt forwards.

Loud

The index finger points towards the ear and makes forward circling movements at the side of the head.

Love

Cross both hands over your chest.

Magic (Two part sign)

Hold both hands in an 'O' shape in front of your body with the backs of the hands facing upwards. The hands move forwards as the fingers spring open.

Make

The right hand fist strikes the left hand fist in a circular motion.

Manger

Cupped hands mime the curved shape of a crib.

Marched

Arms held stiffly down the sides of the body move alternately back and forth to imitate the march of a soldier.

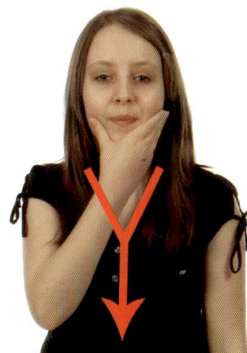

Men

The fingers and thumb of one hand stroke down either side of the chin, to indicate a beard, and then the fingers close onto the thumb underneath the chin.

Message / Tell

Index finger moves forward and away from the mouth.

Monkeys
Hands scratch under the arms like a monkey.

Must
Both 'flat' hands held apart, with palms facing each, other move sharply downwards.

My
Closed fist is held against the chest.

Near
Both hands with index fingers pointing upwards are held apart. One finger remains still while the other moves nearer to it until the hands are touching each other.

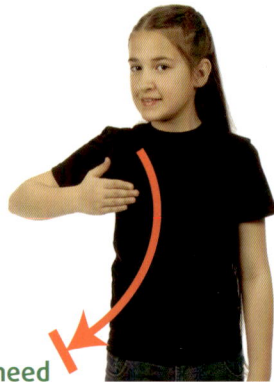

No need
Flat hand with palm facing the body, brushes down the side of the body ending with the palm facing downwards. At the same time, shake your head.

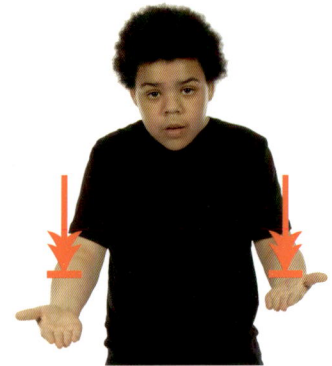

Now /Today
Flat hands, with palms facing upwards, make short downwards movements twice.

Owl
Hold your hands in front of your eyes, bending the index, middle fingers and thumbs of both hands and twist them from side to side twice to show the big eyes of an owl.

Peace
With both hands in an 'O' shape, begin with the tips of the index fingers and thumbs of both hands touching in front of you. Then slowly draw them down and apart.

Pig
A closed hand makes small circles in front of the nose to show the snout of a pig.

Please / Thank you
A flat hand moves away and down from the mouth.

Poor
The tips of the fingers of a 'clawed' hand scratch twice at the elbow of the opposite arm, as if to show the hole in a jacket.

Porcupine
One 'open hand' with fingers splayed, moves backwards across the middle of the head to show the spines of a porcupine.

Rabbit
Hold two 'N' hands held at either side of the head with the palms facing forwards. Twitch the 'ears' by bending the fingers at the knuckles twice.

Safe / Saviour
Blade of the flat right hand, sweeps back towards the body across the palm of the left hand.

Relax
Both fists with the thumbs touching the chest move forward away from the body as the fingers spring open.

Same / Too
Fists of both hands, with index fingers extended and pointing forwards, are brought together so that index fingers are touching side by side.

Sang / Sing / Song
Two 'V' hands move forwards, upwards and away from the mouth in small circles.

Sea
Both 'open' hands, with palms facing downwards, move up and down and apart from each other to show the waves of the sea.

Sent
Index finger pointing upwards, held up and away from the body, moves back down towards the body.

Sheep
Fists, with little fingers extended, draw the circular shape of the horns of a ram at the side of the head.

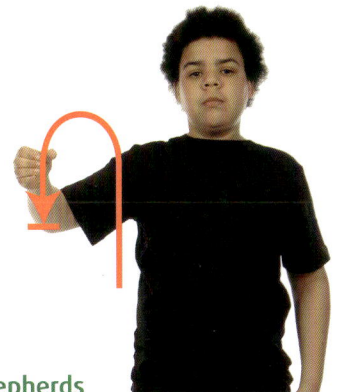

Shepherds
A full 'C' hand, held upsidedown in front of the body, outlines the curved shape of a shepherds crook.

Shine / Shining
Both 'open' hands, with the palms facing each other, make short, twisting movements at the wrists as they move upwards.

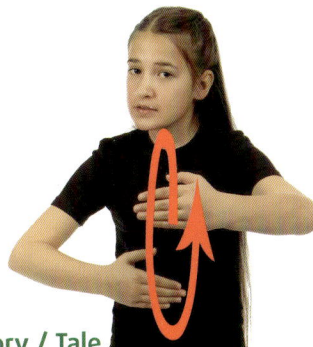

Show / Story / Tale
'Flat' hands held horizontally in front of the body, with the palms facing backwards; make forward circles over each other whilst moving slightly forward and away from the body.

Signed / Signing
With both hands open and palms facing each other, slightly apart, rotate your hands forwards in small alternating circles, so that when one hand is up the other is down and visa versa.

Snow
Both 'open' hands, with palms facing down, move slowly downwards and from side to side with the fingers wiggling to show the gentle fall of snowflakes.

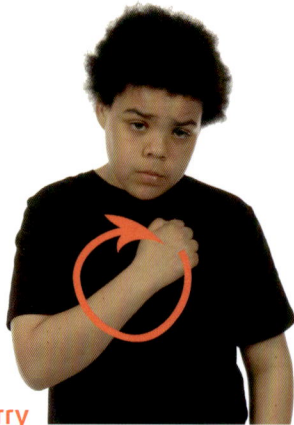

Sorry
Closed hand rubs in a small circle, clockwise, on the chest.

Ssshh!
Press index finger to the lips.

Stable
The tips of the fingers of both 'flat' hands touch together to form a roof.

Star
Look up at a raised 'bunched' hand which then springs open, like the rays of the star.

Stars
Both hands are held above the head. The middle fingers of both hands, open and close against the thumbs as the hands move apart.

Talking
The fingers of both hands open and close against the thumbs, mimicking the movement of a mouth opening and closing.

Think
Tap your index finger against your forehead.

Three
Hold up your index, middle and ring fingers to indicate the number three.

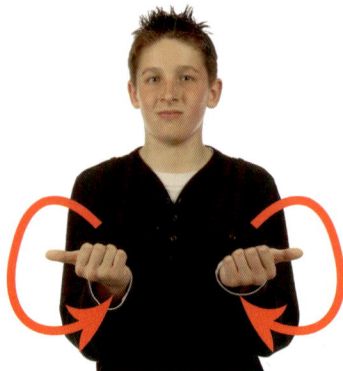

Through (Finished)
Hands clenched in fists with thumbs extended, rotate in small, opposing, sideways circles in front of you.

Time
Index finger points to imaginary watch.

Town
A clawed hand with the fingers pointing downwards makes a short downward movement to indicate a place.

Wait
Fists, with palms facing forwards, make small, opposing, circular movements sideways.

Way
Two 'N' hands, held slightly apart and pointing forward in front of the body, with palms facing each other, move forward to indicate the shape of a path.

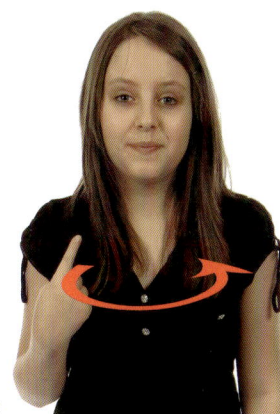

We
Sweep your index finger around in a curve in front of your body, ending up with it making contact with the opposite side of your chest.

Where?
Both 'open' hands held in front of the body, with the palms facing upwards, make small circles in opposing directions.

Who?
Index finger held upright in front of the body, makes small anti-clockwise circles.

Wide
Both flat hands with palms facing each other are held side by side in front of the body and then move apart.

Wise
Tip of the thumb moves from left to right across the forehead.

With
Both flat hands held upright with the palms facing back towards the body. The fingers of the right hand clasp the fingers of the left.

Wondering
Bent index finger makes small circular movements at the side of the head.

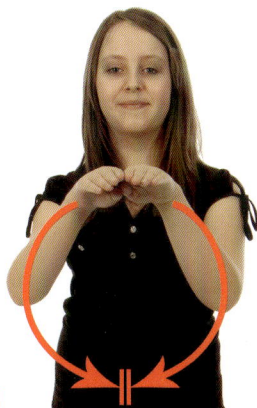

World
Hands outline the shape of the globe.

You're / You
Use your index finger to point at the other person or people.

Script: The shining, signing star

SCENE 1: CHRISTMAS EVE IN A MODERN DAY TOWN

Music: 'Overture' (track 1 on the CD). A child walks across a darkened stage, lit only by a single spotlight, carrying a large placard that reads:

'CHRISTMAS EVE… SALES START 10.00am BOXING DAY'

Four other children, dressed as carol singers and carrying lanterns, walk onto the stage.

The children are on their way home, wrapped up warmly against the cold in coats, hats and scarves.

The children stop in the centre of the stage and shiver with the cold.

FIRST CAROL SINGER:
It's cold tonight

SECOND CAROL SINGER:
I hope there's snow

THIRD CAROL SINGER:
Come on. It's late. It's time to go

The children look up at the sky.

FOURTH CAROL SINGER:
Look! The stars! They shine so bright!

ALL CAROL SINGERS:
I think this is a magic night!

The children exit the stage and the lights dim.

SCENE 2: THE NIGHT SKY

Music: Suggested tune of 'Twinkle, Twinkle Little Star', is playing softly. A child walks across the stage carrying a large placard that reads:

'MEANWHILE, UP ABOVE…'

The stage lights gradually brighten to reveal a group of children dressed as stars. Most of the stars are silver except for one star in the centre of the stage which is a shiny golden colour.

With their arms outstretched, the stars are slowly spinning around to the music, their sparkling costumes catching and reflecting the light. One by one they see the audience, stop spinning and wave.

ALL THE STARS:
Hello!

FIRST STAR:
I know you're wondering who we are

ALL THE STARS:
We are the shining, signing stars

SECOND STAR:
But please, there is no need to go

ALL THE STARS:
Relax, sit back and enjoy the show

THIRD STAR:
We have a story you must hear

ALL THE STARS:
We tell it same time every year!

The stars all cough to clear their throats and then speak in unison.

ALL THE STARS:
Once so very long ago
On a magic night, down below
The Angels of heaven sent a flock of white doves
To the animals of the world with a message full of love

A flock of doves enter from opposite sides of the stage and, taking it in turns, move to the centre of the stage to deliver their lines.

FIRST DOVE:
A girl, far away will have a baby boy

SECOND DOVE:
The baby will grow up and spread peace and joy

THIRD DOVE:
Animals will travel from near and far

FOURTH DOVE:
To see the baby beneath a golden star

The Golden Star steps forward.

ALL THE DOVES:
This star will shine as bright as day

THE GOLDEN STAR:
My light will help to guide the way

ALL THE DOVES:
Animals must go to Bethlehem
And bow to the saviour of all men

ALL THE STARS:
On that cold, dark night above that town
We were those stars just looking down

FOURTH STAR:
So watch this tale, don't fall asleep

FIFTH STAR:
Watch out for talking cows and sheep!

THE GOLDEN STAR:
To see this story we now must go

ALL THE STARS & DOVES:
To the animals' first Christmas, long, long ago

The doves and the stars leave the stage except for the Golden Star who slowly spins towards the back of the stage to watch over the proceedings.

A child walks across the stage carrying a large placard that reads:

'GOING BACK IN TIME NOW... HOLD ON TIGHT!'

SCENE 3: IN A MEADOW

A child walks across the stage carrying a large placard that reads:

'A LONG TIME AGO...... IN A MEADOW FAR, FAR AWAY...'

Children, dressed as animals, are sat in three groups on different areas of the stage.

The groups are: 'The Animals of the Forest' which includes animals such as foxes, badgers, rabbits, monkeys etc.; 'The Creatures of the Sea', fish, seals and crabs etc. and 'The Animals of the Countryside', cows, sheep, pigs and other farm yard animals.

A donkey steps forward to the centre of the stage to speak. After the donkey speaks, each group of animals stands up in turn to say their line.

DONKEY:
Animals from far and wide

THE ANIMALS OF THE FOREST:
From forest

THE CREATURES OF THE SEA:
Sea

THE ANIMALS OF THE COUNTRYSIDE:
And countryside

ALL THE ANIMALS:
All watched the donkey lead the way
To Bethlehem for Christmas Day
The Golden Star helped them along
And as they marched they sang this song

All performers and choir sing and sign the song 'Follow the Donkey':

The owl, the rabbit, the pig, the bat
The badger, the crab, the fish, the cat
All will go to see the boy
And celebrate with love and joy

Follow the donkey
Follow the donkey
Follow the donkey
Don't be late
Follow the donkey
Follow the donkey
Don't you make the baby wait

The fox, the dog and the kangaroo
Camels, birds and elephants too
Cows and sheep come join the line
But watch out for the porcupine!

Follow the donkey
Follow the donkey
Follow the donkey
Don't be late
Follow the donkey
Follow the donkey
Don't you make the baby wait

Three wise monkeys from the east
Will follow the star to join the feast
Each of them a gift will bring
To set before the baby king

Follow the donkey
Follow the donkey
Follow the donkey
Don't be late
Follow the donkey
Follow the donkey
Don't you make the baby wait
Follow the donkey
Follow the donkey
Don't you make the baby wait

Following the Golden Star and the Donkey, the animals dance their way off the stage.

A child walks across the stage carrying a large placard that reads:

'BETHLEHEM, 500 MILES..... WELCOME BREAK, 2 MILES'

SCENE 4: BETHLEHEM

A child walks across the stage carrying a large placard that reads:

'WELCOME TO BETHLEHEM... (NO VACANCIES)... HAVE A NICE DAY!'

Mary, Joseph and the donkey enter. On stage are four innkeepers. Each of the innkeepers is holding a sign with the name of their taverns on them. Mary and Joseph approach three of the innkeepers in turn and mime asking the innkeepers for a room.

Three of the innkeepers shake their heads and sign 'sorry'.

Finally Mary and Joseph approach the fourth innkeeper who is already shaking his head as they arrive.

FOURTH INNKEEPER:
Sorry!
Now please go away.

MARY:
Please, please, please

JOSEPH:
Help us today

FOURTH INNKEEPER:
I know a place where you can go

He points to a stable that contains an empty crib.

MARY:
It's cold and dark!

Joseph shrugs his shoulders.

JOSEPH:
But safe from snow

Joseph, Mary and the donkey trudge off towards the stable.

The Golden Star, the other stars and the doves who were standing in the stable gather around Mary and then slowly move aside to reveal the crib which now contains a baby wrapped in a blanket.

The stars and the doves now move to stand behind Mary and Joseph, who are now sitting on either side of the crib.

In pairs, the animals quietly walk on and sit in groups on either side of the stage.

There is the sound of a fanfare as a red carpet is rolled out from one side of the stage towards the crib.

From opposite sides of the stage, the Shepherds and Wise men slowly walk onto the stage.

The Wise men are dressed like film stars and are wearing sunglasses. They walk along the red carpet waving to the crowds.

The shepherds are not quite so well dressed!

Both the wise men and the shepherds bow to the baby and place their gifts in front of the crib.

THE THREE WISE MEN:
Kings with gold

THE THREE SHEPHERDS:
And shepherds poor

THE WISE MEN & THE SHEPHERDS:
All came to the stable door

Suddenly, a group of sheep rush onto the stage dressed as press photographers, carrying cameras. They crowd round the crib and start taking photographs of the baby and his family.

A child walks across the stage carrying a large placard, made to look like the front page of a celebrity gossip style magazine, that reads:

'BLEAT MAGAZINE: EXCLUSIVE! AT HOME WITH MARY, JOSEPH AND THEIR BEAUTIFUL NEW BABY BOY'

The animals are struggling to get a better view of the baby.
The mouse stands up, shaking his head.

MOUSE:
I can't see for all these sheep

All the animals quickly turn around to look at the mouse and put their fingers to their lips.

ALL THE ANIMALS:
SSSHHH! The baby's fast asleep!

ALL THE STARS:
To the boy the animals bowed
And softly sang.....

MARY:
SSSHHH! Not so loud!

ALL THE ANIMALS:
Sorry we have no gift to bring
But for you this song we sing

All the cast sing and sign together 'You are the Boy':

Little baby asleep in the manger
Watched by angels, safe from danger
Sorry I have no gift to bring
But for you this song I sing

You are the boy
Sent down from above
The king of the world
The bringer of love
You are the boy
Sent down from above
The king of the world
The bringer of love

Following the golden light
I bow to you this magic night
Sorry I have no gift to bring
But for you this song I sing

You are the boy
Sent down from above
The king of the world
The bringer of love
You are the boy
Sent down from above
The king of the world
The bringer of love

(Instrumental refrain)

You are the boy
Sent down from above
The king of the world
The bringer of love
You are the boy
Sent down from above
The king of the world
The bringer of love
The king of the world
The bringer of love

THE KINGS & SHEPHERDS:
We know he is a happy boy
Wise and full of love and joy

MARY & JOSEPH:
Thank you stars for shining bright
We know this is a magic night!

All the cast turn and face the audience and speak together.

ALL THE CAST:
Above them all the stars looked down
On that tiny, happy town
The Golden Star had signed the way
To Bethlehem that Christmas Day

All the cast sing and sign 'See the Golden Signing Star'.

See the golden signing star
See its beauty from afar
Above the stable burning bright
Keeping watch throughout the night
Christmas time its light will bring
Animals to see the king
Guided here from near and far
By the golden signing star

Animals from far and wide
Forest, sea and countryside
Star and Donkey lead the way
To Bethlehem for Christmas day
All are here to see the boy
And celebrate with love and joy
Guided here from near and far
By the golden signing star

See the golden signing star
See its beauty from afar
Above the stable burning bright
Keeping watch throughout the night
Christmas time its light will bring
Animals to see the king
Guided here from near and far
By the golden signing star

All the cast speak and sign the final two lines.

ALL THE CAST:
Now at last our story's through
So Happy Christmas from me to you!

All the cast sing and sign together 'Follow the Donkey'.

A child walks across the stage carrying a large placard that reads:

'THE END - APPLAUSE PLEASE!!'

Everybody waves to the audience.

THE END

Follow the Donkey

from 'The Shining, Signing Star'

Words: Garry Slack

music : Paul K Joyce

2

Bars 20–24 (Voice): Fo - llow the don - key, Don - t you make the ba - by wait_____ The

Bar 21–23 chords: Am D⁷ G

Bars 25–28 (Voice): fox, the dog and the kan - ga roo_ Ca - mels, birds and e - le - phants too_

Chords: C/G G Am/G G C/G D/G G D/G

Bars 29–32 (Voice): Cows and sheep come join the line_ But watch out for the... por - cu pine!

Chords: C/G G Am/G G C D Em

mf *mp*

Bars 33–36 (Voice): Fo - llow the don - key, Fo - llow the don - key,

Chords: D⁷ G

37
Voice
Fo - llow the don - key, Don't be la - te, Fo - llow the don - key, Fo - llow the don - key,
Am
D
G
Piano
41
Voice
Don - t you make the ba - by wait
Three wise mon - keys
Am
D7
G
C/G
G
Piano
p
46
Voice
from the East
Will fo - llow the star
to join the feast
Each of them
a
Am/G
G
C/G
D/G
G
D/G
C/G
G
Piano
50
Voice
gift will bring
To set be- fore
the ba - by king
Am/G
G
C
D
Em
D7
Piano
mf

55
Voice
Fo - llow the don - key, Fo - llow the don - key, Fo - llow the don - key, Don't be la - te,
G
Am
D
Piano
mp
59
Voice
Fo - llow the don - key, Fo - llow the don - key, Don - t you make the ba - by
G
Am
D7
Piano
63
Voice
Fo - llow the don - key, Fo - llow the don - key, Don - t you make the
G
Am
Piano
66
Voice
ba - by wait
D7
G
Piano

You are the boy

from 'The Shining, Signing Star'

Words: Garry Slack

music : Paul K Joyce

Lit - tle ba - by sleep in the man - ger, watched by an - gels safe from dan - ger

Sor - ry I have no gift to bring but for you this song I - sing

You are the boy sent down from a - bove, the

2

16

Voice: king of the world, the brin-ger of love, You are the boy sent

Pno. [C] [G] [Am] [D⁷] [G] [C]

19

Voice: down from a-bove, the king of the world, the brin-ger of love

Pno. [D] [G] [C] [G] [D⁷] [G]

23

Voice: Fo-llow-ing the gol-den light, I bow to you this ma-gic

Pno. [G] [Bm/F♯] [Em] [G/D] [Cmaj⁷]

27

Voice: nigh-t, Sor-ry I have no gift to bring but for you this song I___

Pno. [D⁷] [G] [B/F♯] [Em] [G/D] [C] [D⁷]

31

Voice: sing _____ You are the boy sent down from a - bove, the

Pno.: G | G C | D G

35

Voice: king of the world, the brin-ger of love, You are the boy sent down from a - bove, the

Pno.: C G | Am D⁷ | G C | D G

39

Voice: king of the world, the brin-ger of love

Pno.: C G | D⁷ | G

43 Instrumental

Voice:

Pno.: G Bm/F♯ | Em G/D | Cmaj⁷ | D⁷ | G B/F♯

4

See the Golden Signing Star

from 'The Shining, Signing Star'

Words: Garry Slack

music : Paul K Joyce

Magical ♩ = 70

Voice / Piano / Pno.

Lyrics:
See the gol-den sign-ing star, see its beau-ty from a-far, a-bove the sta-ble bur-ning bright, keep-ing watch through-out the night, Christ-mas time its light will bring, a-ni-mals to see the king, gui-ded here from near and far, by the gol-den sign-ing

2

22
Voice
See the gol - den sign - ing star, see its beau - ty from a - far, a -
(8)
G C D
Pno.
mp
24
Voice
bove the sta - ble bur - ning bright, keep - ing watch through - out the night.
(8)
G D7 G
Pno.
26
Voice
Christ - mas time its light will bring, a - ni - mals to see the king,
(8)
C G D G7
Pno.
mf
28
Voice
rit.
gui - ded here from near and far, by the gol - den sign - ing star.
rit.
(8)
C G D D7/C G
Pno.

Index of signs